Exhale

A collection of inspirational readings.

By

Julie W. Hubbs, M.S.

and

Contributing writers

ISBN: 978-1-795781-60-2

Hubbs, Julie W.

EXHALE. Julie W. Hubbs, M.S.

Cover designer: Julie W. Hubbs, M.S.

Cover photographer: Dana Woodworker-Negri.

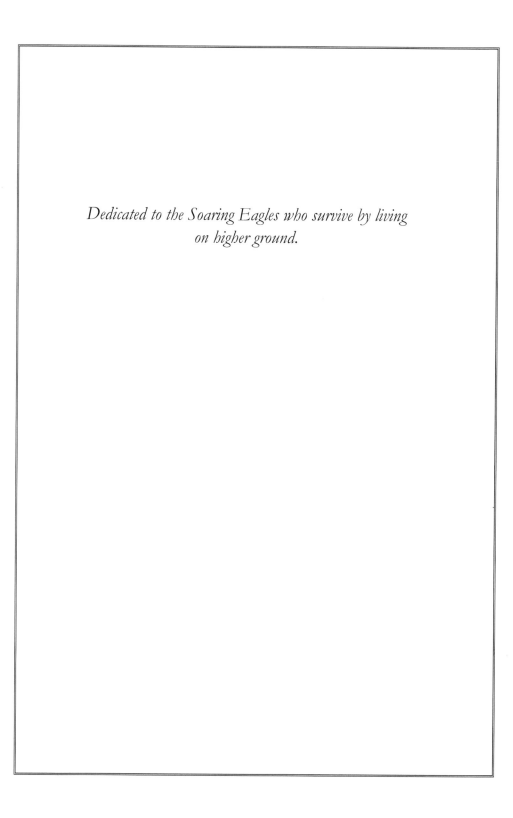

Dedicated to the Soaring Eagles who survive by living on higher ground.

*I*ntroduction

I have compiled a series of readings in the hope they will awaken people to new insights about themselves and their relationships with family, friends, and colleagues. The readings will encourage people and serve as a source of inspiration. Whether your heart is crying for comfort, protection, or direction, the material is a reminder you can always be the best version of yourself.

Exhale is an moving collection of motivational, inspirational, and enjoyable readings, some of which are written by men who were incarcerated for over 20 years. In times of hardship or self-doubt, these readings can be just the pick me up that gets people motivated and back on track.

-Julie W. Hubbs

Kindness

Show more kindness than seems necessary because the person receiving it might need it more than you will ever know. Show it often and expect nothing in return. Kindness is more than just being nice. Kindness is about recognizing and believing another person deserves to be treated with care and concern.

Being kind does not mean you are soft or weak. Instead, it is a sign of confidence. Being kind requires courage and strength. By being kind, you take the risk of being taken advantage of.

When people know you are genuinely kind and considerate, they more readily accept it when you deny a request and have to say no. They understand you are making decisions based on the greater good for everyone involved, and decisions are not being made arbitrarily.

Every act of kindness creates a ripple effect because kindness is very contagious. People genuinely value experiences over material things. They often want to spend time with you exchanging stories about life.

In the words of Maya Angelou, "People will forget what you did, they will forget what you said, but they will never forget how you made them feel."

"Goodness is about character, integrity, honesty, kindness, generosity, moral courage, and the like. More than anything else, it is about how we treat other people."

–Dennis Prager

"Do not follow where the path may lead. Go instead, where there is no path and leave a trail."

-Anonymous

*L*oving Kindness

Kindness packs a sack lunch for a child, but love adds a personal encouraging note inside.

Kindness provides a computer for a child, but love creates a rule to limit the child's use of the computer.

Kindness give a child a bedtime, but love takes the time to tuck the child in with a hug, a kiss, and a story.

Kindness grocery shops for food, but love cooks the family's favorite meal.

Kindness sends a card, but love adds a special note.

Kindness does household chores, but love sets out a bouquet of fresh flowers and a good smelling candle.

Kindness is pouring a glass of milk, but love adds a homemade chocolate chip cookie.

Kindness tells a child to exercise, but love goes outside and plays with the child.

Kindness is doing what is decent, but love is taking the extra time and effort to make others feel special.

Loving kindness is being tender, loving, and considerate of others.

"Not feeling accepted can be a symptom of not accepting yourself. Don't seek attention of others. Find your own approval."

–Jerry Corsten

"About all you can do in life is be who you are."

-Rita Mae Brown

Power*Up

Power*Up is a group for middle school kids in grades six, seven, and eight. Finding their true voice and head-heart-gut alignment is the goal.

A sixth-grade girl brought an issue to group. She told the boys she wanted to play basketball with them. A boy, without missing a beat, told her to (blank) off.

Her friends pressured her to tell the teacher about the profanity. When we asked about her head response she said, "I am very mad and upset." She shared her heart was hurting not because of what the boy said but because her friends were "peer pressuring" her. Her gut reaction was disappointment. Her friends put so much pressure on her she started to believe if she did not tell the teacher her friends would not like her anymore.

After processing in group, she decided to ignore the peer pressure and work on her head-heart-gut alignment. She wanted to find her true voice and make the best decision for herself. She made the decision to think before she acted.

The next week when she came back to group she reported, "Things are great! While I was thinking and aligning myself, someone else told the teacher."

"Drama can be an addiction. It's so so sneaky. Jealousy- all of those things can really send you in a lot of different crazy directions."

—Christian Slater

"Find a place inside where there's joy, and the joy will burn out the pain."

-Joseph Campbell

Drama Queen

A lifestyle full of too much drama can be exhausting. Check yourself out and determine if you are the creator of drama or the drama victim.

People can be attracted to dramatic situations without being aware of it. Chaos may become the norm for the majority of your relationships. You and your friends may often make a big deal over things and unnecessarily create constant turmoil.

Learn from drama and make positive changes. You're not powerless. Get the drama out of your head by not relying on assumptions, by being direct when you talk to other people, and by avoiding drama queens.

Don't feed other people's drama because it increases stress, ruins friendships, and wastes your time. Consider making new friends who are not drama queens. Communicate clearly, be direct, deal with the real issues, and eliminate confusion.

Do all of these things and you will likely have less drama in your life.

"We buy things we don't need with money we don't have to impress people we don't like."

—*Will* Rogers

"A budget is telling your money where to go instead of wondering where it went."

-*Dave Ramsey*

Money

Having a healthy relationship with money is a great goal. Many people work hard all week, get their paychecks, and wonder where did all my money go? If you too ask yourself this question, you are probably in debt. If you are spending more than you earn, you are probably in debt. If you spend to impress other people, you are probably in debt.

Debt can cause stress and anxiety. It is time to take a closer look at your spending habits and start the process of getting out of debt. Just because you can make the payments does not mean you can afford the purchase. Credit can create a false sense of freedom. Higher credit card limits can create the illusion of more financial freedom.

You have the power within you to change your spending habits and to begin getting yourself out of debt. Your legacy can either be you owed on everything, or everything you had you owned. It is your choice how you want to spend your money. Make a budget because it will allow you to spend money without guilt. When your money is assigned to specific areas, that is when you are in charge.

The reward for living debt free is reduced stress, reduced anxiety over money, and having more funds available for everyday living and for future goals.

"To avoid criticism, say nothing, do nothing, and be nothing."

—Aristotle

"Let me never fall into the vulgar mistake of dreaming that I am persecuted whenever I am contradicted."

-Ralph Waldo Emerson

*C*amouflage

Don't look at me. Shh! I am not saying anything. Talking leads to people seeing and hearing me. The chances of me being hurt, disappointed, or judged are far too great. It's what always happens when I let people in. It's safer for me to stifle and ignore my voice rather than say anything that can be used against me.

When I get involved with people there are always negative consequences; therefore, I taught myself to merely exist. I camouflage myself so no one can see me, hear me, or hurt me. I'm invisible, even to myself.

However, there is nothing good about living a camouflaged life. It makes the world small, trust towards others nonexistent, and you will live life from the sidelines.

We were meant to have full lives and not merely exist in a camouflaged state. Challenge yourself to make life a journey of experiences and good relationships. Find your voice and learn how to use it. Be remembered in a way that impacts those around you in a positive manner, and never again live your life on the sidelines in a camouflaged state.

Rob

"Hope is a renewable option: If you run out of it at the end of the day, you get to start over in the morning."

–Barbara Kingsolver

"All that I am, or hope to be, I owe to my angel mother."

-Abraham Lincoln

Hope

Hope is an optimistic state of mind that is based on an expectation of positive outcomes with respect to events and circumstances in one's life or the world at large. Being hopeful allows people to expect with confidence and to cherish a desire with anticipation. People with hope tell themselves, "I can do it!" Hope is not a wish. It is a reason for expecting better.

Hope lifts people up.

Hope inspires us.

Hope is unbeatable.

Hope is unflappable.

Hope is a light that shines bright.

Don't be afraid to let hope lead your way.

"The more rules you have about how people have to be, how life has to be for you to be happy, the less happy you're going to be."

—Anthony Robbins

"Learn the rules like a pro, so you can break them like an artist."

-Pablo Picasso

Thimbles and Reservoirs

Farmers study past weather patterns to predict what the current season will hold for their crops. People often try to do the same thing with their personal relationships. They look at their relationships and study their past to determine if history will keep repeating itself.

As a boy, I was acutely aware of the potential and probability of getting hurt by my loved ones. I tried hard to survive in a self-protection mode. I withheld my trust and became extremely guarded, not letting anyone get close to me. I learned how to predict when the hurt or disappointment was coming, and being guarded made the hurt and disappointment be less painful.

Now I am a grown man who realizes people can only give what they are able and capable of giving, nothing more and nothing less. I believe it is selfish of me to demand affection, love, and trust from people who are not capable of giving me the love, affection, and trust I want from them.

When people love me today, whether it's as small as a half full thimble or as large as an overflowing reservoir, I receive the love graciously. I understand they might just be giving me what they are able and capable of giving, nothing more and nothing less.

Shawn

"You can make more friends in two months by becoming interested in other people than you can in two years by trying to get other people interested in you."

–Dale Carnegie

"Coffee is a hug in a mug."

-Anonymous

*J*ava with Julie

Are you lonely even though you're busy all the time? Have your gadgets become your best friends? Is there too much white noise in your life? Are you the person who is constantly busy, yet never has time to make new friends or nurture old relationships? I was that person. It took a while for me to understand being busy and having lots of friends was not the same as having good relationships. In fact, most of the time the opposite was true.

Many of us have trained ourselves to stay busy 24/7, and believe the more friends we have on social media the less lonely we will be. Sometimes that's true; for example, when I had knee surgery a few years ago, I was thankful for my gadgets. The nights were long and lonely, and I used the internet to keep connected to the outside world. Day or night, I could log on to see what was happening outside my room. My gadgets kept me busy, connected, and less lonely throughout my rehabilitation.

However, after rehabilitation, I craved human connections and genuine friendships. I looked at my list of friends and found people I genuinely wanted to get to know better. That's when the Java with Julie coffee breaks originated. I started inviting five friends to my kitchen table for a 30 minute, give or take, coffee break. We'd drink coffee, visit, and allow no phones at the table.

The coffee breaks are such a big hit, I now get text messages saying, "Hey, I need a Java with Julie fix. When are you free?"

"You cannot be lonely if you like the person you're alone with."

–Wayne Dryer

"I really believe that some things happen for a reason, and they make you a better person."

-Divyanka Tripathi

*B*etter

In the last 10 years, I am proud to say I have raised a significant amount of money for charity. I teach anger management, addiction recovery groups, criminal impact, victimization impact, and various adult education courses. I teach veterans about how to manage their PTSD, and I am a counselor and a life coach. I have earned two college degrees and a business certificate in five years. I have a loving family, good friends, and great ties to the community. I dream, hope, love, and dare to be a better person every single day. I love encouraging other people to be their best selves.

Yet, for the past 25 years, I have been called despicable, worthless, and no good by people who do not know me, have never really met the real me, and who will never really know the real me. I am in prison, and I have been given the label of convict, inmate, prisoner, despicable, worthless, no good, and told I will never amount to anything.

Yes, I am a prisoner, and I did all those things mentioned earlier while serving time in prison. Why, because that's is the real me. My past does not define me. I am proud of who I have grown into. I know my truth, and I love who I am. When people try to degrade and label me, I remember my truth. I am not what they label me. I am better because I am me.

Aaron

"You know you're in love when you can't fall asleep because reality is finally better than your dreams."

–Dr. Seuss

"Every time I see you, I fall in love all over again."

-Anonymous

*B*eing in love feels really easy when you know it's right.

You know love is right when:

You don't have to make outlandish plans, because just being out together doing nothing feels perfect.

You talk about dreams you want to accomplish in the future without realizing you are both discussing the future.

You know everything feels right when you are together.

You don't want to be separated even for a few days because when you're apart you really do miss each other.

You say I love you because it is the truth and not because you're just supposed to say the words.

You care for your loved one during an illness, and it doesn't feel like a sacrifice.

You go the extra mile, and it doesn't feel like an imposition.

You know you two have something special.

You want to be together when the world has knocked you down.

You feel safe like nothing bad can happen when you're in each other's arms.

You reach for each other first thing in the morning to make sure what you have is not a dream.

"In three words I can sum up everything I've learned about life: it goes on."

–Robert Frost

"My mission in life is not merely to survive, but to thrive; and to do so with some passion, some compassion, some humor, and some style."

-Maya Angelou

You can tell the character of a person by how that person acts once that person has experienced defeat. My days are cold, the kind of days that are so cold my gray shadow shivers as it matches me stride for stride across snowy grounds. All the years I remember and every year yet to come, are supposed to be filled with these cold days. Those years I remember as yesterday are snow beneath my feet, crunched beneath my heavy boots, and raked by my still shivering shadow.

The world breathed in my essence and exhaled my shame. They said I was no good and had no future. They said I was nothing. They labeled me defeated before I had a chance to win. As consolation, they gave cold days for my participation.

Crunch, I keep walking, alone with my thoughts and wondering at the taste of defeat. Strange, I did not know that defeat tasted like the burning fire of desire. I did not know that defeat tasted like the cool perseverance of a glacier moving across the land. I did not know it tasted sweet like the memories of home. I should not be tasting, but I do.

I learn. I hope. I care. I love. I dare to be. If this is defeat, then beat me down and mock my worth. Challenge my pride. But know you only make me stronger. From ashes to fire, from fire to life I burn. My cold days are my fire.

You can tell the character of a person by how they act once they have experienced defeat. My character stands tall, because heat rises.   Aaron

"If you want to know what a man's like, take a good look at how he treats his inferiors, not his equals."

–J.K. Rowling

"No act of kindness, not matter how small, is ever wasted."

-Aesop

When a man was visiting a local restaurant, he noticed there was a chicken salad sandwich and a chicken sandwich on the menu. The restaurant asks patrons to circle their choices for sandwiches, chips, and drinks on a slip of paper that gets turned in to the cook. The man wanted the chicken salad sandwich, but he absentmindedly ordered the chicken sandwich.

When the waitress brought him a chicken sandwich, he immediately insisted the waitress had made a mistake. He said he had ordered a chicken salad sandwich. Many waitresses would have picked up the order slip to prove the customer had made a mistake. Instead she apologized and took the sandwich back to the kitchen and returned with a chicken salad sandwich.

As the man was finishing up his lunch, he looked down at his order slip and noticed the mistake had been his. As he went to the cash register to pay, he apologized to the waitress and offered to pay for both sandwiches. The waitress said, "That is not necessary. It makes my day that you have forgiven me for being right."

"You have control over three things in your life- the thoughts you think, the images you visualize, and the actions you take."

–Jack Canfield

"You control you."

-Anonymous

Control

You will never be able to control another person. You can only control yourself and your own behavior. Because of this, it's best to invest energy into something you can control, and that is you.

When everything feels out of control, that is the time when people often try to control the impossible. Remember, you will never be able to control other people. There are things in this world you will not ever be able to change. There will always be 24 hours in a day. Holidays will always come and go. Children grow up and move on. You can't change the way you were raised. Controlling how others drive isn't going to happen. You will never be able to control your teenager's mood swings or your two-year old's tantrums. People dying, loved ones getting terminally ill, and tragic accidents are out of your control. Don't waste your energy even trying to control these things, because you will never succeed.

Instead, invest your energy into what you can control, your thoughts, your visualizations, and your actions.

"A mentor is someone who sees more talent and ability within you, than you see in yourself, and helps bring it out of you."

–Bob Proctor

"The delicate balance of mentoring someone is not creating them in your own image, but giving them the opportunity to create themselves."

-Steven Spielberg

*Q*ualities of a Good Mentor

Listening: Listening is often more important than talking. Listening allows the people to formulate their thoughts and feelings. When the mentor is quiet, this gives other people time to feel their feelings and turn those feelings into words. Sometimes the words have never been spoken out loud before. When the mentor is quiet and is truly listening, intuitive questions surface allowing people to more clearly understand their problems.

Communication: Mentoring is a two-way process. While listening is crucial, so is being able to interpret and reflect back in ways that remove barriers, pre-conceptions, bias, and negativity. Communicating with no personal agenda and suspended judgement enables trust and meaningful understanding on both sides.

Understanding: A good mentor understands thoughts, heartfelt emotions, and gut feelings of what is being said and what is not being said by the person. Working with people's personal anxieties, feelings, thoughts, hopes, and dreams is a huge responsibility. When the mentor is trusted the person will open up.

"Darkness cannot drive out darkness: only light can do that. Hate cannot drive out hate: only love can do that."

—Martin Luther King Jr.

"Status will get you nowhere. Only an open heart will allow you to float equally between everyone."

-Mitch Albom

*O*pen Your Heart!

1. Resist the urge to react with anger.

2. Avoid closing yourself off.

3. Get out of your comfort zone.

4. Make new and different friends.

5. Be open to new information.

6. Close your eyes and allow thoughts to settle.

7. Listen actively, suspending judgement.

8. Explore other cultures.

9. Trust yourself.

10. Check your ego at the door.

11. Practice silence.

12. Send out love to others.

13. Pray, mediate, and quiet your mind.

14. Open your heart and receive love.

15. Keep hope alive.

"To be yourself in a world that is constantly trying to make you something else is the greatest accomplishment."
–Ralph Waldo Emerson

"Don't compromise yourself. You're all you have."

-John Grisham

*B*eing Me

As a young man, I was easily manipulated and controlled by my friends. I had low self-esteem, and I needed praise from my peers to feel loved. I pushed my family aside because my friends meant more to me. I did everything my friends told me to do, and this ultimately turned me into a monster. I became a person even I didn't recognize.

Years later, I woke up and realized if I wanted to be a good person, I needed to find my own voice and quit being other people's puppet. I needed to make some serious life changes because I wanted to live a life that benefited me, not my friends. Letting go of my old friends wasn't easy, but when I finally quit caring about what they thought of me, my life began to turn around.

I learned how to take control of my own thoughts and actions in a positive way, and I pushed myself to grow. I got an education. I attended self-help groups, and I learned how to put my broken pieces back together. I stopped thinking as a child and began making conscious decisions as a man.

Now I am a genuine, caring, authentic, vulnerable, transparent, and proud man because I made myself grow into being the very best version of "Being Me."

Anthony

"No one can make you feel inferior without your consent."

-Eleanor Roosevelt

"You never know how strong you are until being strong is the only choice you have."

-Cayla Mills

Unbroken

I was punched, kicked, and deprived of sleep. I was mentally and verbally abused almost every day for three months. The days of being told, "You're too slow!" "What are you, stupid?" "You're weak!" were taking a toll on me. I wanted to walk away at times. For the first few weeks, tears were my nightly companion. I almost quit one day. I got angry and tired of the abuse, so I made up my mind to push through. I knew I wasn't any of the things I was being called. I knew they were trying to break me. I'd be damned if I was going to break.

When I graduated from basic training and claimed the title of United States Marine, I came to some serious understandings about myself and what I experienced. What I accomplished had nothing to do with my drill instructors. It was about me. I endured and succeeded because I refused to be defined by anyone but me.

As I progress through life, I have encountered many other people who think they have the right to define me and make me feel less than I am. Nobody has that right but me. When I look in the mirror, I love that person. Those who wish to throw verbal stones or act like the iceberg that sunk the Titanic should come look at my mirror. It reflects me. There are no cracks, pits, or distortions, only me unbroken.

Aaron

"My father taught me not to overthink things, that nothing will ever be perfect, so just keep moving and do your best."

-Scott Eastwood

"A problem is a chance for you to do your best."

-Duke Ellington

*D*o Your Best

You can always do your best. Your best is never going to be the same from moment to moment. When you wake up refreshed and energized, your best will be better than when you are sick or tired. You don't have to try to do better than your best. Just do your best every day. As you create new habits, your best will get better over time.

If you always do your best, it makes it impossible to negatively judge yourself. When you are not negatively judging yourself, you will not suffer from guilt, blame, shame, and self-punishment.

Be the best you-you can be every day in every way!

"Success is not final; failure is not fatal: it is the courage to continue that counts."

—Winston Churchill

"Try not to become a man of success. Rather become a man of value."

-Albert Einstein

*S*uccess

My success doesn't look like everyone else's. For years, I tried to make my success emulate everyone else's, and I was extremely disappointed all the time. Finally, when I was able to appreciate my successes in a way I could be proud of, I understood I had to fail a lot to become a successful person.

The word failure is such a disappointing word for me because I heard it all through my childhood and young adulthood. I began looking at the word as the lack of reaching my goals instead of an experience I could use to learn and grow from. Therefore, my fear of failure became a tool for avoiding anything that seemed too difficult or too hard to conquer, and I avoided any new experience where I couldn't be the best right off the bat.

Later in life, I asked myself some hard questions, "How can I ever get better at something if I never take a chance? What is the worst thing that can happen to me if I fail?" I realized trying something new, failing, trying again, failing, and trying again is what makes me a success. Staying in the game, and not quitting is my definition of success.

Whenever I'm afraid of failure, I hear the words of John Wayne whispering in my ear, "Courage is being afraid but saddling up anyway."

Chris

"Believe in yourself. You are braver than you think, more talented than you know, and capable of more than you can imagine."
–Roy T. Bennett

"Fall seven times and stand up eight."

-Japanese Proverb

*I*magined Reality

"You'll never be as smart as other people so why try? Why waste your time trying to learn new things that you'll never be able to do? What you should do is…" Because of statements like these, I spent half my life believing I was dumb. I wasn't blatantly being called stupid, but the message was loud and clear. I was less than capable in most areas of my life.

It took me many years to realize I had come to accept these thoughts and beliefs as my own. I didn't understand they were nothing more than the imagined reality of someone else's inaccurate assessment of me. I took on the story as my own truth, but it was a lie.

I believed I was dumb and incapable until I joined the United States Army, served four years, and was honorably discharged. That experience taught me I am smart, and I am very capable of learning new things.

Now I believe my life has value, and I don't get caught up in other people's imagined reality of who they think I am. I am brave. I am strong. I work on reducing self-doubt because I am good enough just the way I am.

Lee

"Happy is the man who finds a true friend, and far happier is he who finds that true friend in his wife."

–Franz Schubert

"No matter how many years pass by in our marriage, there will be two moments I will love you the most, Now and Forever!"

-TL

My wife she's not fair haired

But she is a real beauty

That's why I call her my little cutie

She cleans, cooks, and sews

Sometimes paints her toes

She hates gloom and doom

Her smile lights up a room

She's good with the money

Her outlook is sunny

Just say when

She'll do the work of ten

She's got ideas and schemes

And plenty of dreams

With a really fine mind

A better friend you'll not find

I have a great life

Cause she is my wife

No one else would do

I love her so true

She is truly the best

You can keep all the rest

"Your core values are the deeply held beliefs that authentically describe your soul."

–John C. Maxwell

"Don't be afraid to give up the good to go for the great."

-John D. Rockefeller

Core Values

Having core values, or a code of conduct, is important. Core values give us a structure for living and making decisions. I have a few core values I try to live by most of the time. Notice I said "try" and "most of the time." I am not a perfect person. I am always a work in progress, and I mess up. That is part of being human. We make mistakes. When I know what my core values are for myself, it's easier to identify what went wrong when I messed up. If I don't have a clue what my core values are, I am lost not knowing in which direction I need to go.

- I am congruent, my words and behaviors match.
- I make decisions when my head, my heart, and my gut are aligned and are giving me the same message.
- I act like who I hang out with, so I hang out with who I want to act like.
- I give more than I take.
- I strive to have integrity.
- I laugh at myself and at life.
- I am kind to myself and try to be kind to others.

"It's hard to be a diamond in a rhinestone world."

–Dolly Parton

"True friends are like diamonds, bright, beautiful, valuable, and always in style."

-Nicole Richie

*P*recious Metals

A metal is deemed to be precious when it is rare. The most popular are gold and silver, but there are many other metals that are precious and take rank in the top six. For example, platinum, palladium, ruthenium, and rhodium are also rare precious metals.

Every Friday morning for the past several years, my Precious Metals woman's group has met for an hour to encourage and strengthen each other. We connect face to face for spiritual, emotional, and mental renewal. We give each other hope in extremely difficult situations, and we help simplify our stressful lives.

Giving advice or trying to "fix" is not allowed. Instead, we encourage and support each other to find our own best answers and solutions. We encourage one another to be the best version of ourselves by aligning our heads, hearts, and guts, remembering to use our voices, taking time to breathe, and more importantly remembering to exhale.

My fellow group members are intelligent, charming, loving, are able to forgive their own flaws, and are focused on making the world a better place. A more precious and rarer group of women you will not find.

"It's not about perfect. It's about effort. And when you bring that effort every single day, that's where transformation happens. That's how change occurs."

–Jillian Michaels

"Strive for continuous improvement, instead of perfection."

-Kim Collins

*P*rogress Not Perfection

If you want to be a positive person, you have to make an effort to create a positive life. Merely wishing and hoping you will be a positive person does not make it happen. Everyone has days when they are angry or grouchy. But if you are negative more than you are positive, then bravo to you for wanting to make a change. Many people don't think they are negative even though their family and friends say things like, "Now don't be so negative" or "Hear me out before you toss out my idea," or the classic question, "Are you ever positive about anything?"

Personal awareness is key to making changes. Identifying and then writing down your negative comments or negative thoughts in a journal is important. You may have been negative so long you don't even realize how negative you are.

Make a new commitment every day to be positive. Start small and practice often. Understand you will never reach a level of perfection because negativity can creep back in when you are not paying attention to your words and thoughts. Set out each day to replace negative behaviors with positive behaviors, and replace negative self-talk with positive affirmations until this practice becomes your habit. It's all about progress not perfection.

"Learn from the past, set vivid, detailed goals for the future, and live in the only moment of time over which you have any control: now."

–Dennis Waitley

"One cannot and must not try to erase the past merely because it does not fit the present."

-Golda Meir

When It Rains

I have often heard the saying, "When it rains, it pours." I am sure many of us have heard this saying, and attach negative connotations. We often believe that when bad things happen, they happen in droves. While it is easy to reconcile this with what we have experienced, the opposite can also be true, though frequently overlooked.

We look at the past and the bad things that have happened in our lives and it feels like a constant torrential storm. Unfortunately, this tends to color our views and expectations of the future, and we look forward with apprehension and fear.

Instead shift your thoughts and focus on the good that rain can bring. Rain signifies renewal, fertility, and change. Rain represents plentiful crops. The rain cloud is a magical symbol to promote good prospects in the future. I look at the rain now with fresh eyes and say, "Let it rain until it pours."

Shawn

"We don't develop courage by being happy every day. We develop it by surviving difficult times and challenging adversity."

–Barbara De Angelis

"A moral being is one who is capable of reflecting on his past actions and their motives, of approving of some and disapproving of others."

-Charles Darwin

*R*eflections

If you stare into my eyes, look deep. Go past the reflections of today and into the memories that define not just a person, but also an awareness.

There's a little boy standing in front of a dam. The dam is holding a lake of emotions. The little boy stares at the dam and notices it's cracked and leaking. He wonders if he should plug the leak or let the water wash over him. He is not scared, just cautious.

There's an older boy swimming in the lake by himself. He's filled with adventure, curiosity, and a broken heart. A young man runs around the lake, chased by his own shadow. It radiates painful memories, opportunities lost, and despair.

An older man sits on top of a mountain overlooking the lake. He cradles the shadow as he watches his younger self. He's happy. He sees what he was, and the mountain he climbed to become who he is. He's aware of himself and the power he has. That power is love.

If you stared into my eyes, you'd see the love I have for you and would never be alone.

Reflections in a mirror.

Aaron

"Remember that not getting what you want is sometimes a wonderful stroke of luck."

–Dalai Lama

"Acceptance and tolerance and forgiveness, those are life altering lessons."

-Jessica Lange

When you want something and you get it, that is an amazing feeling. But when you don't get what you really want, it can feel terrible and sometimes causes feelings of anger and bitterness. Maybe it was the person in high school or college who you knew you could not live without. Perhaps you were passed over for that perfect job you spent your entire life training for. Did you spend hours praying for the outcome you knew was right for you, but it never came true? If so, you are not alone.

All of us will experience many highs and lows throughout a lifetime. Sometimes the lows are the catalyst needed to make changes to be the best version of yourself. Getting through the lows gives us confidence to handle future big hurdles.

So feel what you need to feel and then move on. When something doesn't happen the way you think it should happen, maybe you were spared an experience that would not be good for you. Feel your feelings, cry, scream, pout, or share your sadness with a friend and then move on.

Don't get discouraged because you did not get exactly what you wanted and how you wanted it. Try being genuinely hopeful for a better outcome next time. Working through difficult disappointments usually causes us to become better and stronger.

"Be the reason someone **SMILES** today."

—unknown

"Share your smile with the world. It's a symbol of friendship and peace."

-Christie Brinkley

Smile

A smile has the power to change a mood or attitude. My mother had the best smile. It was so bright she'd light up a room when she walked in. She always wanted people to feel included. She'd say, "You never know what a person is going through or has gone through. Maybe you could be a bright spot in that person's otherwise complicated day."

Years ago, I was terrified to walk into a room full of strangers. A beautiful woman smiled and invited me to sit at her table. I loved her energy and kindness and told her so. She thanked me, and her smile got bigger. When I left the meeting, I thought about how easy a mood or attitude can be changed with a smile.

When I am invited to speak before groups, I always scan the room looking for that one person with the best smile. Why? Because that smile changes my mood, helps me relax, and makes me feel like I belong. A smile from someone, even a stranger, helps calms my nerves.

Smiles are contagious and cause a ripple effect. It's hard to frown when someone's flashing you a beautiful smile. Smiles are something that should be worn often, so surround yourself with people who brighten your day because the world is always a better place when people smile.

"Life is a series of natural and spontaneous changes. Don't resist them; that only creates sorrow. Let reality be reality. Let things flow naturally forward in whatever way they like.

-Lao Tzu

"The world as we have created it is a process of our thinking. It cannot be changed without changing our thinking."

-Albert Einstein

Change

It is difficult for me to understand people who say they want to live independently, yet are not willing to use the tools available to ensure an independent lifestyle. An example would be refusing to use a walker, cane, or electric cart because they don't like "the way it looks." They tell me they don't want to "look" like they need help. But they do need help, and using these tools will help to keep them living independently longer.

I have a 78-year-old client who walks a mile to have her session with me. She arrives wearing a fashionable pink sweat suit or a pair of cute, colorful jeans. She almost always is sporting a baseball cap with sequins, and her make-up is applied perfectly. As she enters the building with her walker, she never forgets to tell me, "I don't need this thing, but I'll be damned if I am going to fall on that rough sidewalk and break something."

I understand my client's attitude. She doesn't want to fall because she enjoys and wants to continue to live independently. However, there are people who see this as "giving up" or "giving in." For me, I see the exact opposite. In reality it is merely moving into a different developmental stage. With each new decade of life things can and probably will shift a bit, and adjustments need to be made.

I recently had a birthday. It was not a "milestone" birthday but a birthday just the same. I am not as agile as a 20-year-old, nor adventurous as a 30-year-old, or as ready to take on the world as a 40-year-old. I am not "giving up or giving in." What I am doing is adjusting to where I am emotionally, spiritually, and physically. I plan to eat healthy foods, exercise every day, continue with activities that challenge my mind and body, laugh with my family and friends, and enjoy life to the fullest for a long time.

When the time comes for me to need a cane, walker, or electric cart permanently, I hope I just do it. However, it would not surprise me if I too, at first, resist these changes.

*V*oiceless No More!

In *It's Your Life, Live It, Love It!* I tell you the story of my life and the problems that I have overcome with the hope that you too can overcome any challenges in your life. As a child I grew up believing all people were loving and kind. What I learned in my early twenties is that some people are just mean and cruel. As a young woman, I did not have the knowledge, skills, ability, or self-confidence to stand up to bullies who were trying to control me. I made up excuses for their bad behaviors because I needed to believe there was something good in everyone. Perhaps I needed to see something good in everyone so I could feel better about my own life.

I mistakenly trusted everyone, and this nearly cost me my life. Although my physical scars have long ago healed, because of my past abuse I can still become anxious when I am feeling trapped or controlled by another person. The difference now is I have life skills that allow me to make healthier choices for myself, and I am no longer a victim without a voice. Available on Amazon.

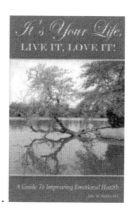

"Never let anyone belittle your efforts to better yourself. Let them stand back or stand aside, but you move forward no matter who tries to stop you."

—Toni Sorenson

"It's not who you are that holds you back, it's who you think you're not."

-Hanoch McCarty

*B*elieve in Yourself

Recently, I was hired by an organization whose mission statement matched my passion. I was excited to get this great job because I had just been released from prison after serving 31 years. It was easy to faithfully serve the organization because I wholeheartedly believed in the program. However, one day, I was unexpectedly fired. Getting fired from a job I loved severely hurt my heart and sat heavily on my soul. I can honestly say my spirit was nearly crushed.

Without warning, I was at a crossroads in my life, and I had many moments of doubt. I called upon the strength of my spirit and relied on my belief that God had a greater purpose for me. It was those two things that lifted me out of the pit of my own self-doubt. I made up my mind to survive and thrive in spite of this downfall. I decided to rise above my circumstances and set my mind on being a success.

With this resilience of spirit, I rose like a phoenix from the ashes and secured a job with another employer who, I am happy to say, is genuinely happy to have me as part of their team.

I followed my heart, recognized my self-worth, and did not allow anyone to crush my spirit.

Charles

I adore his smile

I cherish his hugs

I admire his heart

But most of all…

I love that he is

My Son

*M*odern Day Effects of War on Mom

I grew up in a home with a father who read and studied everything he could get his hands on regarding World War II. In addition, he had two brothers who served in the Army during that war. Because of this I learned a few things by reading his books and listening to his stories. I was most intrigued by the communications between the soldiers and their families.

I heard and read about wives sending love letters to their husbands, mothers sending letters of care and concern to their sons, fathers sending letters expressing pride, and children sending stories and pictures to their dads. Most letters were mailed with hopes they would actually reach the hands of loved ones. Families did not know if their letters arrived safely to the recipients, and at times they did not know where their soldiers were located. I am guessing prayers were prayed and candles were lit as extra precaution to help ensure the safety of their family members and the safe return of all those fighting in the war.

The first time my son was sent to the war in Iraq by the U.S. Army, I was prepared to write letters of care, concern, and support. I was expecting to wonder if my letters would reach him. I was prepared to not know where he would be located. I purchased candles to put in my window to light his way home, and I prayed for the safe return of all those fighting in the war, especially my son.

During that first deployment, I received phone calls with a bit of an overseas delay, but the sound was very clear. I woke up to e-mails on the computer and received little gifts in the mail. I remember saying to my husband, "This is great! It's like he is just down the street." I also remember my husband saying, "I don't know." That is all he said even though I tried to get him to elaborate on his thoughts and feelings. I remember thinking, what does he know that I am missing?

One morning on New Year's Day, I received a call from a female soldier we know. She called to wish everyone a Happy New Year. She was calling from Iraq, and with the time change her New Year's Day was coming to an end. She was right in the middle of expressing how much she missed home when there was the sound of a loud explosion in the background. She said in her sergeant's tone of voice, "I have to go!" I said, "Wait. What was that noise? Was that a bomb?" "Yes!" she said. "I have to go. Tell everyone hi and I love them." With that the line went dead, and there was no further communication for the next several weeks.

As I replaced the phone in its cradle, I had a horrible knot in my stomach. "Was she safe, was the base safe, were they under attack, were people being hurt?" There were no answers to my questions at that time. Months later when I saw her and asked about the explosion that went off while we were talking on the phone, she couldn't even remember the event. She said, "Oh, there are explosions going off all the time over there. Who knows what was happening on that day?"

As my son prepares to leave on his sixth or seventh deployment, I too am preparing for his departure. I know I will talk to him on the phone, and there will be an overseas delay. I know it's possible a brutal sand storm may come up without warning, and he might have to hang up abruptly. I am preparing to put our conversation on hold while a helicopter or two or three lands right outside his tent. I am preparing to hear loud explosions when we talk on the phone. I know he might write that he needs an extra homemade blanket from Mom because of the extreme temperature changes from day to night when he's freezing. But most importantly, I am preparing to expect the unexpected.

"Like a rainbow, you bring color to ordinary places.

Like a sunset you add brilliance.

Like a river, you know the way.

With the patience of the forests, you wait for your dream.

And like the most special flower in the garden.

You grow stronger and more beautiful every day."

-Ashley Rice

*D*aughter-in-Law

I love you more than you will ever know, and I want nothing but the very best for you. I love sharing all that comes your way because you are the best daughter-in-law on the planet.

My hope is that as the years go by we will become even closer than we are today. You are more than a daughter-in-law. I think of you as my daughter.

"Discard anything that does not spark joy."

-Marie Kondo

"We learn the process of emptying out, cleaning house both within and without."

-Brenda Shoshanna

*C*lutter Bust

I am making an appointment with myself to clutter bust my guest room. I've been "meaning" to do this for a while, but it just hasn't happened. I had other more pressing things I wanted to do, or had to do, or thought I had to do. Today, I have a date with myself and my room.

Have you ever felt blah as soon as you stepped into a cluttered room? Clutter can actually cause stress hormones to build up in your body. I feel so much more relaxed when my house is in order.

Set small achievable goals. Start with the room you spend the most time in. Then focus on one area at a time, perhaps the bedroom closet or a drawer in the kitchen or a shelf in the garage. Start small so you don't get overwhelmed. That little bit of tidying will energize you.

SMART skill approach:

- **S**et a goal. I want to clutter bust my guest room.
- **M**onitor progress. I will be working from 1:00 to 4:00 p.m.
- **A**rrange my world for success. I have empty boxes to take items to charity or to the trash can.
- **R**ecruit support. Ask for help.
- **T**reat yourself. After clutter busting, I will buy fresh flowers, a terrific smelling candle, or a new book.

"Life is ten percent what you experience and ninety percent how you respond to it."

-Dorothy M. Neddermeyer

"Behavior is what a man does, not what he thinks, feels, or believes."

-Emily Dickinson

*B*ehavioral Drift

If you are drifting back into old unhealthy behavioral habits don't panic! A healthy dose of fear is a good thing. It lets you know something is wrong, and you need to make a change before things get too out of hand.

Panic can lead to unhealthy binges, quitting exercise routines, smoking, illegal drug use, and other unhealthy behaviors that are used to soothe.

In the movie *Chasing Mavericks*, the surfer saw a shark and began to panic and splash. His trainer told him, "Don't panic, be alert, breathe, and slowly swim away to safety."

When I have behavioral drift, I pay attention to my behavior, take many deep breaths, and I slowly step away from the candy dish, chips, cake, or whatever is catching my attention during the drift. I tell myself, "You are not going to gain a 120 pounds back in one week. Don't panic. Accept the healthy fear and get back on track RIGHT NOW!"

"I've always enjoyed seeing the world through the eyes of children."

-Neil Sedaka

"My family, my husband, my son, my daughter-in-law, my grandson, my niece, all of them are the most important people in the world to me."

-Julie W. Hubbs

*L*andon

Landon, Landon he's our boy

Mom and Daddy's pride and joy

Landon, Landon our little man

He'll win your heart as fast as he can

Landon, Landon our spiky-haired boy

Each time at the store he'll find a new toy

Landon, Landon stay around him awhile

He'll win your heart with his cute little smile

Landon, Landon couldn't be finer

He's our little grandson from North Carolina

*G*ianna

Gianna, Gianna she's our girl

She can eat a big ice cream swirl

Gianna, Gianna just for a lark

She loves to go play in the park

Gianna, Gianna is nobody's fool

She's the top student in her Italian school

Gianna, Gianna mama mia!

How much she loves her special Zia

Gianna, Gianna comes to play

Time to leave she wants to stay

Gianna, Gianna in this whole city

There is no girl half as pretty

*C*ameron

Cameron, Cameron he's our boy

He's our family's pride and joy

Very much like his old man

He'll be a big Chicago Bears fan

When he stops playing and his time is free

He might join Mom watching General Hospital on TV

Now the story starts to unfold

On December 30th Cameron turns one year old

On this we're sure we can't be wrong

Cameron is growing to be big and strong

If it is the nicest kid you have in mind

Cameron, Cameron is the boy you'll find

Oh, my goodness and heavens above

For Cameron our hearts are filled with love

"Money often costs too much."

-Ralph Waldo Emerson

"The greatest gifts you can give your children are the roots of responsibility and the wings of independence."

-Denis Waitley

*T*alking to Kids

I was part of a workshop for teenagers at Sacramento City College. The facilitator, who works for Golden 1 Credit Union, asked this question, "What is important to you?" He also asked, "What does money do for you and the adults in your life?" At first the answers were as expected. "I can buy things." "It makes me happy." "I can buy presents, and we could go on a vacation."

As the room grew silent, the adults sitting in the back of the room began to join in. One by one each adult added their words: stressful, complicated, workaholic, struggling, unhappy, divorcing, bill collectors, bankruptcy, and I wish I had more because there is never enough.

The teens were excited and hopeful about money and acquiring more money. The adults were sad, struggling, and unhappy when they were talking about money. This got me thinking. How come the relationships with money are so different between the teens and the adults? Wouldn't it be great if talking about money was often not taboo? I would love to know how many adults discuss money with their children, explaining how and why financial decisions are made for the family.

Noted financial author Larry Burkett says, "Money is either the best or the worst area of communication in our personal relationships."

"The truest help we can render an afflicted man is not to take his burden from him, but to call out his best energy, that he may be able to bear the burden."

-Phillip Brooks

"Find a group of people who challenge and inspire you, spend a lot of time with them, and it will change your life."

-Amy Poehler

Support Team

I love teamwork. Just ask anyone who knows me. I enjoy bouncing my ideas off others or adding my thoughts to other people's ideas. For years, I have heard the expression, "No man (or woman) is an island." What this means to me is, we need each other. I thrive when I have an emotional support team on my side. It makes me feel loved, cared for, connected, secure, and safe. Plus, I laugh more, cry more, and have more aha moments when I am with a team.

My connections to other people create a safety net for me. Having a team allows me to fall without failing. I trust these people enough that I can be my real self with them. I know they have my back. Now that does not mean they will always agree with what I am doing or saying. What it means is they will not, on purpose, throw me under the bus.

I have always said, "You act like who you hang with." If you want to be happy, hang around happy people. If you want to be nice, hang with nice people. If you do not want to eat so much processed food, hang with people who enjoy planning and preparing healthy meals. In other words, find people who are already behaving the way you want to behave. Let some of their energy rub off onto you. Group energy can be extremely powerful when used for good.

Now finding these people to be a part of your emotional support team is not always easy.

I have a very strict rule about who can and cannot be on my emotional support team. For example, just because someone is family or my best friend does not mean they are my best supporters. I have a dear friend who loves junk food. That friend will not be on my support team because I do not want to eat junk food. My friend's behavior goes against my goals. It does not mean my friend is a bad person, it just means my team members need to be 100 percent supporters of me and my goals.

Again, this does not mean that family and friends will agree with everything I say or do. But they need to support me in reaching my goals.

Once I have picked my potential support team, I ask myself these questions:

Do I trust them completely? Do I feel safe telling them anything? Will they judge me if I fail? If I keep failing will they categorize me as a failure? Will they appreciate my honesty?

I encourage you to get a support team together for yourself. If you do not know people who fit this criterion then take the time to meet people who can and will be there for you. Ask yourself, what three places you can go to start meeting people who can be a part of your team?

*G*rief

It is to be hoped most people go to the grocery store because they need food and other supplies. But sometimes people grocery shop because they are sad, bored, lonely, or believe spending at the grocery store is "OK because we all need to eat." Emotions might be dictating your spending and not just at the grocery store. I have a client who I will call Jenny. Her husband died many years ago. She lives alone and has grown children in the area and claims they are all very close. She also reports that she "still misses her husband terribly."

When Jenny's husband died, she went to the grocery store late at night because she "wanted to be with people." It was comforting to be with others, so she saved the chore of food shopping for the late evenings. She would shop for two because she could not believe her husband was really gone.

In the beginning she believed it was harmless because she was being soothed and always had enough money for groceries. Eventually, Jenny realized she was using shopping as an unhealthy coping mechanism. She joined a support group and soon discontinued her unhealthy behavior.

"Life is really simple, but we insist on making it complicated."

-Confucius

"If the sight of the blue skies fills you with joy, if a blade of grass springing up in the fields has power to move you, if the simple things of nature have a message that you understand, rejoice, for your soul is alive."

-Eleonora Duse

Keeping It Simple

The late Vince Lombardi, coach of the Green Bay Packers, was once asked why his championship team ran such a simple set of plays. He said, "It's hard to be aggressive when you're confused." I often wonder how many people are confused due to the complexities in their daily lives. I know I get confused merely listening to the goals some people hope to accomplish in a day, let alone in a week, month, or a year.

My life is a system. That is what I have been telling myself and my husband for years. In reality, I live my life with a creative plan that allows me to simplify things. I weed out, delegate, and eliminate all activities that don't add to my goals. I try hard to handle things in the moment. Here is an example: today I made a Costco run and purchased supplies for my household. Most of the items I bought are stored in the garage. When I returned home, I backed my pickup truck into the driveway and began cleaning the garage. This included, sweeping, shop vacuuming spider webs, wiping down the washer and dryer, cleaning the outside fridge, and pulling items off the shelves that needed to go to charity. As I unloaded and put away the supplies from the bed of my pickup truck, I began loading the items I had collected for charity.

After taking a 30-minute coffee break outside with my husband on this warm sunny January day, I drove down to Goodwill and gave them my donations. The entire process took about two hours. Now remember, I had a 30-minute relaxing coffee break while sitting outside in the sunshine conversing with my husband.

I simplify my life by combining tasks. In just two hours the garage, refrigerator, washer, dryer, floors, laundry room area rug, and shelves got cleaned. The shelves got organized, my supplies were put away, and items were taken to charity. Most importantly, I enjoyed relaxing in the sunshine while visiting with a loved one.

You might be thinking, "This does not sound simple to me, sounds like a lot of work." I will let you in on a secret. When you have a plan that is "strong and simple," there is less confusion; therefore, the task is more likely to get done. It is hard to stay motived when you are confused. When you simplify your life, it gathers focus. The more you can focus on your goals, the more motivated you feel. The more motivated you feel the more things you will accomplish.

My mother always told me and my sister, "Everything in your room needs to have its own place or else I'm getting rid of it." It was her way of making sure we cleaned our rooms while keeping inventory of our belongings. Figure out your system and decrease the confusion in your life. Remember to keep it super simple.

*J*oyful

I have always said, "You act like who you hang with." If you want to be negative and nasty then hang with negative, nasty people. However, if you want to be cheerful, friendly, and nice then find people who are supportive, friendly, and are genuinely nice people to hang out with. Before you know it, they will bring out the best in you.

Strengthen your friendships by being a positive person. When a friend gets a promotion, celebrate with him or her. Happy people take genuine joy in accomplishments of their friends. According to Sonja Lyubomirsky, PhD, happiness researcher, you're 25 percent more likely to feel joyous if you have a happy friend who lives within a mile of you. Happiness is contagious, so make it a goal to find some happy people to hang out with.

"The healthiest competition occurs when average people win by putting in above average effort."

-Colin Powell

"I've always considered myself to be just average talent and what I have is a ridiculous insane obsessiveness for practice and preparation."

-Will Smith

Average

The highest achievers many times shoot for the moon, but even when they miss and land among the stars, they are OK.

We need goals that are not too high and not to low, and that can be tricky. For example, if your child is reading a book and knows every word on the page, the book is too easy. If your child is reading a book and doesn't know five words on the page, the book is too hard. Dr. Sylvia Rimm says, "High achievers usually have moderate goals." Goals need to be not too hard, and not too easy.

In the above example, it would be fun to have our children reading medium level books and enjoying them without the frustration of having to be "the best" or the fear of being "the worst." I say it's time to make being average OK.

"Getting stress out of your life takes more than prayer alone. You must take action to make changes and stop doing whatever is causing the stress. You can learn to calm down in the way you handle things."

-Joyce Meyer

"Relaxation comes from letting go of tense thoughts."

-Frances Wilshire

*C*almness

Research shows that faking calmness when you are over anxious can actually calm you. So, the next time your anxiety is extremely high, simply pretend that you are calm and relaxed by taking slow deep breaths and lowering your voice when you talk. Within five minutes your mind and body should be calmer.

I think we should do this often and before our stress gets to the "over anxious" stage. I don't know about you, but I need all the calmness I can get. I am going to take a break and do some deep breathing right now. How about you?

"The beauty of a woman must be seen from her eyes, because that is the doorway to her heart, the place where love resides."

-Audrey Hepburn

"I think a hero is any person really intent on making this a better place for all people."

-Maya Angelou

*P*urple Heart

Is it a coincidence that my friend Nancy, a police officer wounded in the line of duty, picks a key out of a large bucket with the word HEART on it? I think not!

She was awarded a Purple Heart. Nancy has a strong heart, a tender heart, a good heart, and a very loving heart. Sometimes her heart even gets broken. But she never gives in, and she never gives up.

There were 200 keys in the bucket. She could have picked any number of keys, but without even looking she picked the key with the word HEART on it. I remember the look on her face when she read the word on her key. She was stunned into silence.

Nancy has more heart than most and is brave beyond belief. When I think about The Keys to Being the Best You-You Can Be, I know in my heart this was the perfect key for my friend Nancy.

Thank you for your service sweet girl. There will always be a special place in my heart for you.

"Every now and then go away, have a little relaxation, for when you come back to your work your judgement will be surer. Go some distance away because then the work appears smaller and more of it can be taken in at a glance and a lack of harmony and proportion is more readily seen."

-Leonardo da Vinci

"The vacation we often need is freedom from our own mind."

-Jack Adam Weber

*R*elax on Vacations

Do you ever really relax, or do you just think you do? I have asked myself this a million times. It seems like I have been on the go my entire life. My mom said I have been on the move, exploring since I was in the crib.

My head seems to always have a thought, a plan, or a goal that is getting ready to be put into action. I have decided to make some changes in my life. Now when I am spending time with my family or on a vacation, I soak up every minute of that time. I do not hide behind my camera trying to capture every moment on film.

A new study in the Journal of Psychological Science suggests that putting the camera down improves your memories of the vacation later on. I am living proof and will tell you why.

My husband and I spent six weeks in Europe. Halfway through the trip I deleted about 1,200 pictures from my camera by accident. As you can probably guess, I was horrified and very angry at myself. I just wanted to sit down and cry, and then I wanted to go home because I was feeling sorry for myself. This was a bit irrational I know, but my feelings were genuine.

As soon as I got over the shock of having lost my "once in a lifetime" European vacation pictures, it was actually very freeing. I did not have to worry about taking pictures of everything because half my trip pictures were gone. It forced me to be in the moment. I created moments in time and memories with my husband that will be remembered forever.

Yes, I have some pictures from my European vacation, and since I have been home I have not looked at them once. However, on many occasions we have talked about experiences we had that were not captured on film. Putting the camera away led to more enjoyable and memorable experiences.

My thoughts, plans, and goals for future years are to not have thoughts, plans, or goals. In other words, I will be in the moment and soak up my experiences as they come into my life. When I sit down to read a book, I will actually read the book and only think about the plot, the characters, and nothing else.

Fake It till You Make It!

Sometimes when I am in a crowded room and I am supposed to be networking, I get filled with self-doubt and just want to disappear into the wall. I have learned when this happens what I need to do is make myself bigger. I position myself to take up more space.

Body language experts say an "expansive posture activates a sense of power and makes others think and believe you are in command and are confident." Have you ever heard the phrase "fake it until you make it?" Well, sometimes that is me.

I can get very nervous when I am part of a crowd. So, when my nerves kick in, I stand with my hands on my hips, place my legs shoulder-width apart, take deep soothing breaths, align my head, heart and gut, and say it like I mean it. For sure I cannot be the only nervous person in the crowd.

"*Alzheimer's caregivers are heroes.*"

-Leeza Gibbons

"*To us, family means putting your arms around each other and being there.*"

-Barbara Bush

*A*lzheimer's Caregivers are Heroes

Communication Techniques:

- Encourage conversations. Give them time to respond.
- Use good eye contact. Provide gentle touching.
- Give simple instructions. Use their name.
- Don't use baby talk.
- Be aware of your tone of voice.

Caregiver Tips:

- Ask for one thing at a time.
- Create daily routines.
- Reassure them that they are safe.
- Don't argue with them.
- Don't try to reason with them.
- Try not to show anger or frustration.
- Give pacers room to roam.
- Use humor to redirect.

How to Distract:

- Have them listen to music.
- Get them dancing.
- Have them fold clothes.
- Have them rock a baby doll.
- Have them set the table.
- Encourage humming.
- Take them on a walk.
- Give them a healthy snack.

"The best way to not feel hopeless is to get up and do something. Don't wait for good things to happen to you. If you go out and make some good things happen you will fill the world with hope, you will fill yourself with hope."

-Barack Obama

"Once you chose hope, anything is possible."

-Christopher Reeve

*L*ife Coaching at Folsom State Prison

Who knew that an invitation to an Old Folsom State Prison Gavel Club meeting by a local Life Coach would lead to a new training course getting started for the men at Folsom? After much encouragement and some shameless begging, Coach agreed to teach the inmates of Old Folsom life coaching.

The first class began in May 2017 with every seat being filled by Gaveliers. The second class was filled with facilitators from various groups, and the four following classes were open to the general prison population.

The feedback from participants has been abundantly positive, and many more men are curious about what life coaching is and are waiting to get involved.

At first, we had no idea what life coaching entailed. We thought it was helping others get through life with more confidence. Boy, were we way off! As men we want to "fix" things. We want to "give advice," and we want to "make things better fast." Coach Hubbs dispelled that type of thinking. She helped us align our own heads, hearts, and guts by helping us to be our authentic selves.

She wants us to be the best version of ourselves. Coach Hubbs, with her direct and personal style, makes everyone participate. She has a witty and heartfelt style that keeps the class interesting and helps participants feel safe enough to get involved.

Anthony.

"If you alter your behavior because you are frightened of how your partner will react, you are being abused."

-Sandra Horley

"There is no exercise better for the heart than reaching down and lifting people up."

-John Holmes

*D*omestic violence is often used to describe physical abuse of women by men. Physical abuse includes pushing, slapping, punching, hitting, shoving, hair pulling, arm twisting, choking, breaking bones, and even killing. Acts of violence are designed to control, hurt, and physically harm a partner.

Domestic violence also comes in the form of emotional and verbal abuse. Emotional abuse is intended to degrade, humiliate, and demean another person. It is meant to make people feel bad about themselves and their abilities.

Another abuse that is seldom talked about is social abuse. This is where the abuser enforces social isolation and or social controls over the partner. The victim is not allowed to have social contact with friends and relatives. The abuser limits what the partner does, whom the partner sees, what the partner reads, and where the partner goes or doesn't go.

- Are you being physically, emotionally, verbally, or socially abused?
- Does your partner make light of the abuse? Are you being controlled by your partner?
- Do you get intimidated when the abuser looks at you when angry?
- Does your property get destroyed?
- Does the abuser display weapons?
- Are you afraid to leave?

- Are you made to feel guilty?
- Does the abuser threaten to take your children away?
- Have you been bruised, had your bones broken, been bitten, or experienced any other injuries?
- Are you feeling anxious, depressed, or keeping dangerous secrets?

If you answered yes to any of these questions, I urge you to reach out for help.

National Domestic Violence Hotline
www.thehotline.org

■■■

On the next few pages are a listing of the groups

About Progress Not Perfections offers.

About Progress Not Perfection

_Empowering people to make life changes, increase self-esteem,
and strengthen self-confidence._

Our goals are always to empower our clients to make life changes, increase self-esteem, and strengthen self-confidence. For years we have been conducting weekly workshops covering: values; confidence building; "I" statements; reducing shame and guilt; job interview preparation; general household budgeting; reframing thoughts; identifying feelings; making good decisions; and using healthy communication. The following is a list of our workshops.

1. Power*Up helps middle school children find their inner voice and verbally defend themselves against peer pressure and bullies. We meet weekly in area middle schools and teach kids how to express their feelings and learn how to work in effective teams where everyone is heard.

2. Silver Metals helps women find their inner voice, protect themselves from getting into or returning to situations of domestic violence and emotional abuse. Goals are to increase self-esteem and confidence while learning how to communicate effectively during difficult situations.

3. <u>Diamond Strings</u> helps couples find their inner voices, helps them connect or reconnect, helps stop emotional or physical abuse, and helps them to strengthen their relationships to preserve the family unit and reduce the possibility of divorce.

4. <u>Soaring Eagles</u> A training program that prepares incarcerated individuals to successfully re-enter society.

5. <u>Take Flight</u> helps veterans adjust to being out of the military and helps inmates adjust to reentering society. We cover building relationships, various styles of communication, anxiety, expectations, fears, embarrassment, PTSD, and how to adjust to the world after being away from family and friends for extended periods of time.

"Be kind to others wherever and whenever you can."

—Julie W. Hubbs, M.S.

Follow Coach julie_w on Instagram, Twitter

and on her Blog @

www.AboutProgressNotPerfection.com

This is not the end.

It's the beginning.

Made in the USA
San Bernardino, CA
27 January 2020